Write Blog Posts Readers Love

A Step-By-Step Guide

by

Henri Junttila

Table of Contents

Introduction

I've always wanted to write.

I've always wanted to reach out and inspire people through my words.

Blogging seemed like the perfect platform to do that, but for a long time, I didn't know what to do or how to do it. I didn't know how to write blog posts that my readers would love.

When I started, I was confused, overwhelmed, and lost, but I eventually learned what works and what doesn't, and today I run a 10,000+ subscriber blog over at WakeUpCloud.com.

I didn't build a popular blog through influential connections or a magic wand. I started from scratch. I'm not talented or special. I don't consider myself an expert. I'm just a regular guy from Scandinavia who felt inspired to write.

You're reading this because you have something inside of you that you want to share. You feel drawn to write blog posts that touch souls. And that's exactly what you'll learn to do in this book. This book is what I would've wanted when I was starting out, because it would've saved me years of frustration and overwhelm.

Here's a taste of the questions we'll answer in this book:

- How can you uncover your true blogging style (and feel confident while writing blog posts)?

- What's the secret to attracting a loyal and supportive audience?

- How do you keep your readers coming back day after day by telling inspiring stories?

- What are the key factors in coming up with unlimited blog post ideas?

- How can you write faster while producing higher-quality blog posts?

- What kind of blog posts are the most popular (and how can you use them)?

- Do you really need a writing process to build a popular blog?

- How do you eliminate writer's block once and for all with a simple technique?

- Is there a way to stay motivated when you want to give up and when your energy wanes?

This book contains everything I've learned while building a blog that gets tens of thousands of visitors every single month.

With this book, my goal is to share the techniques that currently work best for me. Everything you're about to learn comes from my personal experience. I've taught these techniques to others and they get results. Fantastic results.

Now you can discover how to write blog posts that readers love, which will help you build a thriving blog that makes your heart sing.

How to Use This Book

You'll get the most out of this book if you implement what you learn. Each chapter contains one or more action steps that will help you, well, apply the information.

You don't have to apply the information perfectly. Remember, this book contains what works for me, and what works for me may not always work for you. So feel free to modify the information. Use what you learn as a springboard for your own ideas and methods.

Enjoy the process of discovering which of the tips and techniques work best for you, because it's when you have fun, and when you don't take things so seriously, that you make the fastest progress.

You may want to read through this book once before going back to the chapters that excite you the most. Whatever you do, take action and use this information, because it will make a difference in how your writing and blogging is received.

As you get better, you'll build an audience, get thank-you emails from readers, and your confidence will soar—but only if you take action.

Now let's begin with our first chapter.

Uncover Your Blogging Voice

What separates one blogger from another? Is it because they have something unique to say? Is it because they are blessed with talent? Maybe.

But in most cases the answer is no. So what sets them apart? Why are some people attracted to Steve, while others prefer Charlie?

It's their writing voice, their style, and their perspective. People want to hear your opinion. They want your worldview. They want to get inside your head.

You don't have to try and find your blogging style, you just have to embrace who you already are. You have to share what you feel to be true. You have to share how you view the world.

In this first chapter, we'll take a look at the what, why, and how of uncovering your unique blogging style. It's already in you, which is why I use the word uncover.

Ready? Let's dive in.

What is a Writing Voice?

A writing voice is confidence. It's courage.

It's the boldness to share what you are afraid to share. It's having the courage to share your mistakes, secrets, and stories. I'm not talking about sharing everything, but sharing what's relevant and helpful to your reader.

Some will like what you have to say, and some won't. My writing doesn't resonate with everyone, and that's fine. The people that it resonates with, it does so deeply.

Why Looking for Your Voice is a Mistake

When you try to "find your writing voice," you get stuck, because that's impossible. It's like trying to find a needle in a haystack, but without the needle.

You have to realize that you already have a writing voice. You just have to use it with courage. You will discover who you are through writing. Your writing will touch thousands. But only if you have the courage to start.

You have to be ruthless. Don't let your doubts, fears, and insecurities stop you. You have to keep writing even when that voice in your head says that you're no good and that no one will ever like what you put out.

What others think is none of your business. What matters is that you feel inspired to write.

How to Uncover Your Writing Voice

I don't write the way I wrote five years ago. In three years, I probably won't write the way I do now. I'm constantly improving.

I don't consider myself an amazing writer. Heck, I'm not even a native-English speaker. I was born in Northern Sweden, in the Arctic Circle, yet here we are.

When you start blogging, you'll run into fears. You'll make excuses. You'll feel like you can't do anything right. But so what?

To uncover your voice, you have to write. We all have to deal with doubt, insecurity, and fear. The difference between writers and non-writers is that writers write anyway.

There is no magic formula to success. There is only the willingness to write in both good times and in bad times.

For me, uncovering my voice has been about letting go of fears that stop full self-expression. I still have doubts and fears, just like anyone else, but I write anyway, because I know from experience that my readers want to hear my viewpoint.

The point I'm trying to make here is that your readers want you to stand for something. They want to hear your opinion. They want you to share what you feel to be true. They want you to be you.

We all have an inner critic. Learn its patterns. Observe how it undermines you, but don't fight it. Let it be. Let it fuel your writing. Channel your energy, and beware of one thing…

The Big Mistake: Death by Comparison

With the internet, you have the whole world at your fingertips. You get to compare your insides to someone else's outsides.

You can look at someone's edited life on Facebook and think you're not good enough, when in reality you're only seeing a tiny part of their life.

You can read an article in the New York Times that's been edited and polished for months, and compare it to your blog post.

You can visit blogs that have been around for decades and get discouraged because you'll "never get there."

When you compare your writing to someone else, you're doing yourself a disservice. Your writing doesn't have to be like someone else. It has to be you. It has to be your truth.

So stop comparing, stop wondering what if, and stop feeling sorry for yourself. You're here to be you, so the only measuring stick you need is your own improvement. If you're moving forward, making mistakes, having fun, and learning, you're on the right track.

What If Your Writing Sucks Right Now?

If you're just starting out, your writing may not be, well, all that great. Mine certainly wasn't when I began.

When you learn anything, you're not going to be the best, and when you compare yourself to others who've been writing for decades, you feel even worse.

Focus on improving your writing. Focus on getting better instead of trying to strive to an impossible ideal. Focus on enjoying yourself because it'll come through in your writing.

When I look at my writing from five years ago, it's horrible. When I look at my writing from just one year ago, I'm flabbergasted.

I've been published on some of the biggest blogs online, yet I still ask myself: "How did I ever even get my articles accepted?"

There will always be doubt, but you can still keep writing, because that's the only way you'll produce blog posts that your readers love. I'm scared from time to time, but I refuse to stop, because this is what I love to do.

What Great Blogging is All About

I don't claim to be a great writer. I just write the way I write. I love writing.

Great blogging comes down to having the courage to stand for something. It comes down to sharing your truth and your worldview.

You don't want the whole world reading your blog, because your writing is not for everyone, it's for a select group of people.

So stop looking for people's approval. If your perspective clashes with someone else's, so be it.

This is your life. You are the only one with your unique perspective.

It's your job to share it with the world, because people want to hear what you have to say. They want to hear from you, otherwise you wouldn't feel inspired to write.

The Big Takeaway

Your writing is what it is. You can't change that. You can't outthink it by "finding your voice."

You have to start where you are with what you have. Yes, that voice in your head will tell you that you're not good enough, but it doesn't matter.

When you keep putting your writing out there, people will start reading, and some of them will love it. The only thing that matters is that you keep writing.

Always keep writing. No matter what anyone tells you. No matter what that inner voice whispers.

If writing brings you joy, then write, because it is only through writing that you will improve. But you have to be willing to stop believing your own … crap. You have to be willing to embrace the discomfort and just write.

Are you ready to do that? If so, then this book is for you. We're just getting warmed up here.

Action Step

In each chapter, you'll get one or more action steps that will help you implement what you've learned. For this chapter, all I want you to do is write one short blog post of about 300-500 words.

You don't have to publish it. It doesn't have to be refined. I just want you to share, from your heart, what you think about the topic you're writing about.

If you blog about tomatoes, then write about that. There are no rules. What matters is that you write, so write.

Find Your Ideal Reader

When you're at a café having a conversation with a good friend, you rarely run out of things to say.

But when you write, you run into trouble. Suddenly you don't know what to say. Your writing doesn't feel right, and you spend endless hours editing, rewriting, and driving yourself insane.

What gives?

One of the reasons is because you don't have a special someone you're writing for—you don't have an ideal reader.

You see, when you write, you need to write for one person. An ideal reader could be a fictitious person that you've created, it could be an actual reader of you blog, or it could even be a friend. What matters is that you keep someone in mind as you write your blog post.

Why Do You Need an Ideal Reader?

An ideal reader gives your writing power. It gives you something to aim at, much like hitting a nail with a hammer. If you don't know where the nail is, it doesn't do much good to flail around with the hammer.

If you try to write for everyone, you risk writing boring posts. But when you're specific, you hit the nail on the head. Not with everyone, but with the right person.

When you focus on one person, your readers will start to feel like you're talking directly to them. You don't want to write for everyone. You don't want the whole world as your audience. You want the people that are right for you.

How to Create (or Find) Your Ideal Reader

The best ideal reader is someone who reads your blog. If you can't find a real person, you can use a past version of yourself, or you can create an ideal reader out of thin air. Do what you can with what you have.

For example, if at one point in time you were a beginner at growing tomatoes, you could write to yourself. You can think back to what your struggles, challenges, and fears were, and write to that past version of you.

Remember, we're not after perfection, just a person we can keep in mind while writing. Let's uncover a first version of your ideal reader.

Who is Your Ideal Reader?

The first step is asking who your ideal reader is. Factors to consider are:

- Gender
- Age
- Marital status
- Children
- Income
- Likes/Dislikes (movies, books, etc)

Let's take an example: I've just started up my blog about growing tomatoes. I'm not an expert, but I know more than I did a few years ago. I can still remember my early struggles. I didn't know what fertilizer to use or how to keep bugs from gobbling up my tomatoes.

I grab a pen and a piece of paper and I start jotting down a past version of me as my ideal reader. I already know what I struggled with so this is going to be just like going back in time and having a conversation with myself.

Keeping a past version of me in mind while I write while make it easy for me to imagine if I would've had trouble understanding something in my article, and what kind of help I would've needed.

What Does Your Ideal Reader Want?

Next, ask yourself what your ideal reader wants. Your readers will stay because you give them something of value. It could be entertainment, education, or encouragement. Whatever it is, your reader wants something.

To figure out what your ideal reader wants, ask yourself questions like:

- What does he/she ultimately want to accomplish?
- Why does he/she want this?
- What are his/her dreams?

Let's take another tomato blog example: I've just started up my blog, but this time, I don't remember what problems the past version of me had, so I'll have to create an ideal reader.

To do this, I go to my favorite search engine and type in 'grow tomatoes forum' and I look at what people are talking about. I might even start a new topic asking people why they are so into tomatoes.

I'll also visit other tomato growing blogs and peek at the comments. I'll look at who is hanging out there, and I'll try to figure out who the blog owner seems to be writing for.

I eventually discover that people like growing tomatoes because it helps them reduce stress, and it gives them a sense of connection to the Earth.

This clues me in to the fact that I need to keep things simple and avoid overwhelming my reader, because overwhelm causes stress. I need to keep my writing lighthearted and easy-to-consume.

What Stops Your Ideal Reader?

This is the juicy part, because more often than not, people come to your blog to solve a problem. Sometimes that problem is boredom, and sometimes it's not knowing how to grow tomatoes.

To uncover this, ask questions such as:

- What is stopping your ideal reader from getting what they want?
- What problems or challenges does he/she have?
- What frustrates him/her?

Example: I'm starting to understand who my ideal reader is for my tomato growing blog, but I want to understand their challenges, so I go back to the forums and blogs I've found, and I dig deeper. I take notes on my computer. As I keep going, I discover that some of the questions people have are:

- They don't know how to start growing tomatoes
- They have trouble with insects
- They don't know how soil works
- Their tomatoes taste weird
- They want to grow tomatoes inside, but don't know how

My list of potential problems keeps growing and it becomes clear to me that I have to start from the beginning and look at what steps someone needs to take in order to go from knowing nothing to having delicious tomatoes on the table.

I start jotting down all the steps, and I realize that I have more than enough content here to last me for several years. I even have an idea for an online course.

"Won't I Alienate Readers?"

Yes. Some people will be turned off by your blog, but that's a good thing. You don't want the whole world to read your blog. You want the people that are the best fit for you.

Think about your favorite blogger. Think about why you read what they write. It's probably because of something they do, and their way of looking at things, that other bloggers don't. Now imagine if they tried to please everyone. Would you still like them? Probably not as much, right?

When you write for your ideal reader, remember that there are probably millions of people like that in the world, even if your ideal reader is Steve, a 23 year old male, living in Wisconsin, USA, who just started law school.

When you write for Steve, every person like Steve will feel like you're writing just for them. And even people who are almost like Steve will resonate with what you have to say.

However, when you worry about alienating readers, you alienate Steve, your biggest fan.

If All Else Fails …

If you can't come up with an ideal reader, write what you would want to read. Write to the past version of you. If you write about tomatoes, write for yourself when you were getting started.

Imagine yourself having an intimate conversation with yourself that you post for the world to see. This will attract people like you to your blog, because you will be using language that only resonates with a certain group of people, and you will be solving a problem that only a few people need.

This is a good thing, because the more you can target the people you can truly help, the happier they will be, and the more they will spread the word.

What to Avoid

Don't try to come up with the perfect ideal reader. There are no rules you have to follow. Just keeping someone in mind while you write will help you write blog posts that readers love.

You don't have to have the same ideal reader for every post, so feel free to experiment. What you've learned in this chapter is just what has worked for me. Pick what works for you and discard what doesn't.

And above all, remember to have fun. There is no rule that says that you have to take blogging seriously. Play around with your ideal reader and write. You'll eventually figure it out. Your ideal reader may not be perfect. It doesn't matter. Do your best and write. That's how you'll figure this out.

Action Step

Begin by writing down who your ideal reader is. Remember to give them a name. Brainstorm, experiment, and see what comes out. Then write a blog post with your ideal reader in mind.

You don't have to publish this post. All I want you to do is notice how much easier it is to write when you're writing for someone in particular.

If you want, you could try writing a letter to an old friend, just to see what it's like to keep someone in mind while writing.

Tell Inspiring Stories

Your ideal reader, Steve, has arrived on your website about growing tomatoes. He doesn't know anything, and he has no clue about how to get started.

When he lands on your blog, all he sees are posts of you talking about how amazing your tomatoes are and how you've mastered gardening. He feels bad, and he leaves.

This is the fate of most blogs. You see, it's easy to boost your own ego and make yourself feel good. It's not so easy to share your mistakes and flaws, so that your readers will feel inspired to take action themselves.

The key to inspiring your readers is to tell inspiring stories, and that's exactly what you'll learn in this chapter. At the end of this chapter, you'll have a plan for how to create inspirational content that your readers will love.

Let's dive right in.

What does it mean to inspire?

The definition of inspire is: "to fill (someone) with the urge or ability to do or feel something."

One of the biggest complaints I hear from my readers is how overwhelming most blogs are. They give you dozens and dozens of tips, but they don't tell you where to start or what to do with those tips.

Writing inspirational blog posts means understanding that your readers will feel overwhelmed, and that you have to tell them what to expect, what to look out for, and how to get started.

It also means that you're willing to share your own flaws, fears, and struggles, because you understand that everyone has the same fears deep down.

This doesn't mean you somehow change how blogs are structured. Blogs are inherently confusing and overwhelming, because they are filled with content. What I'm talking about is being clear in each post what you want people to do. Now, I don't always do this. This is not something you have to do with every post. It's just something you want to keep in mind.

Why inspire people?

Because your readers will love you for it. It's hard to find someone who is willing to share their own flaws in order to inspire you to take action.

I seem to naturally write inspirational blog posts, because I'm not afraid to reveal that I'm not an all-knowing expert, nor am I a perfect human being.

This in turn makes my readers send me thank-you notes, share my content, sign-up for my newsletter, and buy my products and services. In fact, here's one email I received just a few minutes ago all the way from Spain:

"Hey Henri, just wanted to say that I hope you realize how much you are helping people around the world with this website. I am currently living in Spain, and in a stressful time in my life. Your website helped me a lot today and I just wanted to say thank you and that I appreciate it a lot. I am

sure there are many people who feel the same way as me and feel happier with your writing. Best of luck and continue on!"

Inspiring your readers is not just about making people feel good. It's about realizing that when you help others, you help yourself. When you help your readers reach their goals, you will reach yours.

Now let's take a closer look at how to craft an inspirational blog post.

4 Steps to Crafting an Inspirational Blog Post

Engineering inspiration is all about helping people relate to you. It's about showing that you were once in the same situation and sharing how you got out of it.

As you share how you solved your problem, your readers will be inspired, they will have a-ha moments, and they will be motivated to take the next step.

The downside is that you have to have a story to tell. It could be a personal story, or a story from a friend or a client. This is why I only recommend you start a blog around a topic you're passionate about and where you have a story, because stories make your writing more engaging and inspirational.

Here are the four core steps to writing inspirational posts:

1. Find a Problem

Start by finding a problem. What is your ideal reader struggling with? What's frustrating Steve to bits? What does he wish he wouldn't have to face?

For example: I'm working on my tomato growing blog, and my ideal reader, Steve, doesn't know how to get started growing tomatoes indoors. I've got my problem, and I still remember how confused I was when I was getting started.

2. Identify a Story

In our hypothetical scenario, I remember wanting to grow tomatoes indoors, but I didn't know what I needed to do or what equipment was required. I didn't even know who to ask for help. I also remember a few awkward moments in the store when I was asking the staff for help, so I'll share those to show people that it's okay to not know everything.

I'll also share how I eventually figured out where to get everything. But even when I had everything in place, my tomato plants didn't grow, so I'll share that in order to help set the right expectations. I want to show that there will be challenges, but it's a fun ride.

3. Share Practical Tips

I'll also try to go into as much detail as I can in my story, because this will help Steve visualize what he needs to get and what he needs to look out for.

A good way to do this is to first start with problems and then see if they fit with my story. For example, let's say Steve has three questions regarding growing tomatoes indoors, and they are:

- What equipment to buy
- Where to set everything up
- How to set everything up
- What mistakes to avoid

I now know what I need to focus on in my inspirational story. I'll simply share what equipment I bought, where I set everything up, how I did it, and the mistakes I made. Just sharing the mistakes will tell Steve what to avoid.

As I read through my article, I put myself in Steve's shoes and imagine that I'm brand new to this. I'll think about if something is missing or if I can remove anything from my post to make it simpler.

4. End on a High Note

Last, but not least, I'll end on a high note, and let Steve know that he'll make plenty of mistakes. I'll tell him to remember that he's doing this for fun, so enjoy the mistakes, failures, and screw-ups.

This isn't about growing the perfect tomatoes right away, because that would be boring. This is about making a mess and learning from your mistakes.

So end on a high note. Your story can start with struggle, but make sure it ends on how everything turned out well and how anyone can do this if they're willing to experiment and keep putting one foot in front of the other.

Be on the Same Level As Your Audience

It's easy to try and elevate yourself above your readers. It's great for your ego, but it leaves your readers disempowered. The more you can show them that you've been there and done that, the more you will inspire them.

Inspiration comes down to showing that you once went through the same struggle and that it'll all be okay in the end. It's about giving your readers information, hope, encouragement, and inspiration.

A Quick Summary

Writing an inspirational story is about finding a problem your audience has and telling a story that shows how you once had that problem and how you solved it.

From there it's up to you to decide how detailed you want to make the story. You can always write more articles if people want to know more. Remember, you don't have to give away everything in every post. It's okay, and even preferable, to leave your readers wanting more.

Now let's look at the action steps.

Action Step(s)

The action steps for this chapter are simple:

1. Find a problem your ideal reader has
2. Identify a story where you had the same problem and solved it
3. Tell the story in a post

Don't try to craft the perfect story. Write from your heart, and tell your story. It doesn't have to be perfect to inspire.

Generate Unlimited Ideas

A common fear you may bump into is running out of ideas. What if you run out of things to write about? It makes you so horrified that you don't write anything. It's a self-fulfilling prophecy. When you're afraid of running out of ideas, you run out of ideas.

Worry not, because this chapter will give you access to more ideas than you could ever write about. I'm not hyping this up, because I use the five tips in this chapter myself when I get stuck.

I have pages and pages of blog post ideas. There's no end in sight. The good news is that you are an idea-generating machine. You just have to learn how to tap into your inner genius.

Here's how I do it:

1. Forums, Comments and Q&A Sites

Look at user-generated content, such as:

- Forums in your niche
- Comments on blogs in your niche
- Q&A sites with questions relevant to your blog

You're looking for anything where people are discussing your topic. For example, if I run out of blog post ideas for my tomato blog, I'll look for communities and blogs on tomatoes. If I can't find anything on tomatoes specifically, I'll look for something on gardening.

To find a forum, I'll go to my favorite search engine and type in, "tomato + forum" or "tomato + discussion board."

For Q&A sites, I like to use Yahoo Answers at http://answers.yahoo.com and search for questions and answers. I'll begin by typing in growing tomatoes and any synonyms that come to mind.

As for blog comments, I'll find some popular tomato or gardening related blogs and look at their most popular blog posts. I do this by looking in their sidebar. Most blogs have a section called "most popular posts" or "most commented posts."

Then I'll have a peek in the comments. I'm looking for questions people have, problems they run into, and anything they mention. While I'm at it, I'll also write down the most popular posts on the site. If I notice that a popular post talks about the biggest tomato growing mistakes you can make, I'll probably write my own version covering the same topic.

If you just do this, you'll have plenty of things to write about. Some niches are not as rife with user-generated content. In those cases, you may want to rely on the other tips below.

2. Readers

If you've been blogging for any length of time, chances are that you have an audience. That means you can look at what comments your readers leave.

Do they ask questions? Do you invite them to ask you questions? If not, you should.

You could even send a out a survey using Google Drive and ask three simple questions:

- What's your goal? (As it relates to your blog topic)
- What are your biggest frustrations?
- What are your biggest fears and worries?

This will give you plenty to write about. In fact, doing a survey like this is how I created one of my first products.

But let's pretend I just started my tomato growing blog last month. I don't have many readers. In that case, I'll go to tip #1 above and look at other blogs in my niche and see what information I can find there.

All the information you need is right in front of you. That's one of the perks of the internet. Everything is out there if you know how to find it and use it.

3. Books & Magazines

When you go to Amazon, you see thousands and thousands of books. And on most of those books, you can look inside and see the table of contents.

This means you get to access data that most writers and publishers have spent a lot of time researching.

For my tomato blog, I'll go to Amazon.com and type in "how to grow tomatoes." I'll look for a book that is popular and has many reviews.

Then I'll click on the cover and look inside. Usually there will be a table of contents there. For example, I found one book and in the table of contents I see these topics:

- How to grow tomato plants from seed
- How to select a tomato plant
- How to re-pot tomato seedlings
- How to move tomato plants in your garden
- How to water tomato plants
- How to save your seeds for next season

Just from this one book, I have a whole series of blog posts I could write.

Something else I would do is look at the reviews on Amazon for ideas on what people like and don't like. Doing this on a popular book will give me dozens and dozens of ideas.

Thank you internet, and Amazon.

4. Read

Whenever I read books, I'm overwhelmed with ideas for blog posts. Many people these days don't read books. If you're one of those people, you should try reading. Start small. Read 5 minutes per day in the morning or before you go to bed.

Even if you're reading a Stephen King fiction novel, it will fuel your imagination, and when that happens, you'll find yourself having ideas for your own blog.

When I'm reading business books, for example, I might find someone who puts something in a better way than I do, which sparks an idea for how I could put it better in my own words.

You don't have to read a lot, but make reading a part of your everyday routine. Just a few minutes in the morning and/or in the evening will pay off.

If I'm passionate about tomatoes, I'll probably read books on tomatoes and gardening in general. That alone will produce ideas if I do it on a daily basis. So find a book you've been meaning to read and start reading it for just 5 minutes per day.

5. *Inspiration*

When I'm out and about, I always bring a pen and a piece of paper with me. I like taking notes the old fashioned way. You could also take notes on your phone.

Whatever you do, capture your inspiration when it strikes, otherwise you'll get fewer and fewer bursts of inspiration. If you don't use it, you lose it, as the saying goes.

For example, I might be playing with my son, when suddenly an idea hits me. I'll immediately write down whatever I can. If I'm near a computer (and not playing with my son), I'll dump my brain in a document.

Inspiration is there for a reason. Capture it, and use it to write your posts, because those are often the blog posts that truly touch the hearts of your readers.

You could save your ideas in a document on your computer, but I wouldn't recommend it. I used to do that and all of my ideas ended up getting lost in some digital whirlpool.

My tool of choice is Workflowy. It's a list creation tool that allows you to go endlessly deep into your ideas. It's also extremely simple and fun to use and it syncs across all your devices. You can learn more about it at Workflowy.com.

6. Tap Into Your Past

People love stories, especially when you share some of the biggest mistakes you've made. They want to hear what not to do. Plus, it's entertaining to read about how someone fell flat on their face. Our brains suck up mistake and failure stories like a sponge. It's a learning opportunity.

So ask yourself, what are your biggest:

- Mistakes
- Pitfalls
- Failures
- Lessons

What have you learned during your path to becoming who you are? I freely share my biggest online business mistakes and failures on my blog, and each time, my readers love it.

It also brings me closer to my readers, because it shows them that I'm not superhuman, and that you don't have to be a genius to build a profitable business or grow a popular blog.

So let's once again return to our tomato blog example. I've made plenty of mistakes, and I have stories to tell about plants dying and insects taking over my house.

I have plenty of ideas, so I sit down and brainstorm for 20 minutes. I write down all the mistakes I've made and all the lessons I've learned. This alone produced 20-30+ blog post ideas I could create.

I could also take all of my mistakes and create a list post. The title might be something like, "The 30 Biggest Tomato Growing Mistakes You Must Avoid." Then I could link to each individual article from my list post.

Remember, your mistakes and lessons may not feel special to you, but that's because you already know them. What you know, you should teach. You have to remember that what you find easy, your readers will not.

7. Drill Down Method

I saved the best for last. The drill down method simply means taking one topic and drilling down into specifics. Let's take an example of a topic we both know well—blogging.

Let's say I have an idea for a post where the headline is, "5 Silly Mistakes Bloggers Make."

Most people would write the post and stop there. But with the drill down method, you can take any of the five mistakes in that post and create another post. So let's say one of the mistakes was not having a consistent posting schedule.

I can now drill down into having a posting schedule and create a whole slew of posts, such as:

"How to Keep a Consistent Blog Posting Schedule"
"5 Blog Posting Schedule Mistakes You Must Avoid"
"Why You Have to Keep a Blog Posting Schedule"
"What My Blog Posting Schedule Looks Like"

Do you see where I'm going with this? If I wanted to, I could take any of the posts above and drill down even further. So let's say one of the ways I keep a blog posting schedule is by using a special plugin. The next post I could write could be all about that plugin, how I use it, and where to get it.

This may still be confusing, so think of it like this: Each article you write has subheadings, right? When you drill down, you make one subheading the headline of a new article. So let's say I'm writing an article on my tomato blog. The headline is, "3 Tips to Grow Better Tomatoes."

The 3 tips are:

1. Water regularly
2. Use proper soil
3. Beware of bugs

With drilling down, I'd take one of these tips and focus one entire article on it. So let's say I'd like to drill down on #1: Water Regularly. The headline for my new article could be, "How to Water Your Tomato Plants."

The outline could be:

Introduction
The Watering Mistake Most Beginners Make
How to Water Properly
Example
Summary

I've now drilled down once. I can do this again by making another subheading from the outline above.

Play with this and don't worry about getting it right. Drilling down can be a confusing concept in the beginning, but let it sink in and come back in a few days and re-read this chapter. It'll make sense soon enough.

Ideas Are Everywhere

If you use the tips in this chapter in conjunction with the drill down method, you'll never run out of ideas. And remember, I've only covered five ways to generate blog post ideas. You don't have to look for more. Use what you've learned here and watch your ideas pile up.

The truth of the matter is that ideas are everywhere. What stops you from writing freely are your own fears. You may be afraid of what people may think. You may think that you have to write like another blogger, but you don't.

You are on this planet to be you, so write like you. Not everyone will love your blog, but that's just a sign that you're writing from your heart. Share your experiences and you will attract the right readers.

Action Step

Pick one of the ways above to generate ideas. I suggest you pick the easiest one. If you often browse books on Amazon, go to Amazon, type in your blog topic, and start looking at the table of contents of best-selling books.

Once you're ready, play around with the drill down method. When you do, you'll never run out of blog post ideas again.

But remember to stick to one thing at a time. Play with it for a few days and see what happens.

Craft Compelling Headlines

A headline is a promise you make to the reader. Take a look at the magazine rack next time you go to the store. Most of the magazines live or die based on their headlines.

A great example of this is Cosmopolitan Magazine. They use headlines that pull you in (if you're in their target market, and sometimes even if you aren't). A well-crafted headline gets more attention, clicks, and shares.

Unfortunately, many bloggers skip the headline altogether, thinking that their readers should read their article based on how good the content is. What they forget is that everyone is short on time, which means that the most compelling headline wins.

A blog post with a better headline, but worse content, will get more views than great content with a bland headline. This is why it's important to learn to write headlines that grab your readers by the throat (in a nice way, of course).

Headline writing is an art, like writing, but it doesn't take a lot to start producing above average headlines. You do this by copying what's already working. Copywriters have been copying each other's sales letters, headlines, and writing styles for ages. The reason? It works.

How to Craft a Compelling Headline

When you're starting out, the best way to create headlines is to steal them. In other words, look at headlines that already work and use them to write your own.

At first, you may not be confident with writing bold, attention-grabbing headlines, but as time goes by, your confidence will grow. Do what you are comfortable with, then with each headline, push your boundaries.

This doesn't mean you outright lie in your headline. It just means that you are confident in what you have to offer and why someone should read your post.

Let's take a look at how you can create great headlines on demand:

1. Start a Swipe File

A swipe file is a file where you collect the headlines that resonate with you. If you bump into a popular post that has an intriguing headline, save it to your swipe file. A swipe file can be as simple as a document on your computer.

But I recommend you use something like Workflowy, or Evernote, both of which are free (unless you need more space). I've always been fine with the free versions of both.

So if I'm browsing the web for gardening related information and I happen to come across an article with the headline, "The Best Way to Grow Organic Vegetables," I'll put it into Workflowy under my favorite headlines.

2. *Write Your Headline First*

When I start writing a new article, I write my headline first. That way I know what promise I have to fulfill with my content. It makes planning my post easier.

Writing my headline first helps me stay on topic. If I start writing without a goal, and without a focus, chances are I'll end up somewhere I don't want to be.

But when I write my headline first, I know what questions I need to answer, and I know what idea I want to transmit.

There are times when I won't write my headline first, but they are rare. I'll still come up with a temporary headline just to get a feel for what focus I have for my article. I've found that the more focused my headline is, the easier my blog post is to write.

With my headline, I tell you what to expect in my article. When I know what I've told you, I can focus on making sure I meet the expectations I've set.

3. Practice, Practice, Practice

The more headlines you write, the better you'll get. Pretty obvious, isn't it?

The first few times you write a headline, you'll struggle. It might even take you 20-30 minutes, but it's time well spent.

I've been writing headlines almost daily since 2009. When I started, I wasn't good, but I got better by looking at what other people did and what worked, and by writing a lot of headlines.

I get frustrated like anyone else, but I also know that frustration is a sign that my brain is learning something new. If you get frustrated, take a break and come back the next day when you're refreshed. Push yourself to the edge, but not over it.

Headline Templates to Get You Started

To get your swipe file started, here are a few of my favorite headline templates. Simply replace my words with your own.

"10 Ways to Get More Traffic to Your Blog"
"7 Deadly Mistakes Most Blogger's Make"
"How to Write an Ebook in 30 Days or Less"
"How to Get a Six Pack Even If You're a Couch Potato"
"The Secret to Writing a Best-Selling Book"
"Why You'll Never Find Your Passion in Your Life (And What to Do About It)"
"The Ultimate Guide to Starting a Popular Blog"
"What to Do When You're Afraid of Failure"
"The Best Way to Do What You Love"
"How I Went from 0 to 1,012 Blog Subscribers in 101 Days"
"The Truth About Blogging That No One Wants to Admit"
"What Nobody Ever Tells You About Blogging"
"How to Never Succeed at Blogging"
"What Star Wars Can Teach You About Writing a Book"

Make it a habit to save any headlines you run into that you like. If you keep doing this, you'll end up with hundreds of headlines you can dip into at any time for inspiration.

How to Use Templates

Let's say I wanted to write a post for my tomato blog, and I wanted to use "How to Get a Six Pack Even If You're a Couch Potato," as my template. What I would do is use the same structure (how to and even if) but put in my words.

It might become something like "How to Start Growing Tomatoes Even If You Have No Clue."

Next I could take "10 Ways to Get More Traffic to Your Blog," and turn it into "10 Ways to Safeguard Your Tomatoes from Insects and Bugs."

Another example could be "The Best Way to Do What You Love." I could turn this into a negative and create "The Best Way to Fail at Growing Juicy Tomatoes."

One last example could be taking "What Star Wars Can Teach You About Writing a Book" and turning it into "What My Grandmother Taught Me About Growing Great Tomatoes."

Simply pick a headline template that fits with the kind of article you want to write and let it inspire you to create a compelling headline of your own.

Headline Resources

A few websites that have particularly good headlines are:

- Entrepreneur.com
- Copyblogger.com
- Forbes.com

And you can also check out my blog at WakeUpCloud.com, if you'd like to see how I write headlines.

Action Step

Your first step is to open up a blank document on your computer, write down the headlines you like in this chapter, and that's it. You've started your swipe file.

As you go about your day, throw headlines you like into your swipe file, and use them the next time you write a blog post.

It may be awkward at first, but you'll soon get used to it, and when you do, you'll see more people reading and sharing your blog posts.

Write Scannable Posts

The easier your blog posts are to read, the more likely it is that someone will actually read them, which in turn means that there's a higher likelihood that your readers will share, comment, subscribe, or buy your products or services.

The way you make a blog post easy to read is by making it scannable and by using simple language. This doesn't mean you dumb down your writing. Simple doesn't equal dumb.

You don't have to show off with big words. You have to be understood, and you have to make your ideal reader's life easy.

There are people out there that don't write scannable posts at all, but they are the exception, not the rule. It never hurts to make your posts easier to consume, and learning how to do that will improve your writing.

A big part of writing posts your readers love is being willing to experiment. You have to be willing to throw spaghetti at the wall and see what sticks. I can only share what's worked for me. It's up to you to discover what works for you and your audience.

Here are five tips for writing scannable posts:

1. Write Short Paragraphs

The first way to make your blog post easy to read is to use short paragraphs.

Limit each paragraph to two or three sentences. My readers have told me that seeing a big block of text is intimidating, especially for those who don't read a lot.

When you break your post into smaller paragraphs, there's more white space, and reading feels easier.

What you want to avoid is going overboard, where you end up with a lot of one sentence paragraphs. That's when it becomes awkward. So switch things up, use a one sentence paragraph for emphasis, but default to anywhere from two to five sentences per paragraph.

If you want to see an example of this, take a look at one of my posts: "10 Simple Steps to Building a Thriving Lifestyle Business" (http://www.wakeupcloud.com/10-steps-to-a-lifestyle-business/).

You'll notice that I don't follow the two to five sentence rule religiously. You don't have to, either. Use whatever works and discard the rest. You make up your own rules. Always remember that.

2. Use Subheadings

Look at the way I've written this book, I use chapters and in each chapter I have subheadings to break things up. This creates structure, which is calming for your brain. It also helps you navigate to parts that you find interesting.

It keeps you reading, because each subheading is a small packet of information that you can gobble up and enjoy, much like those small desserts you can't stop eating.

If you want to make your subheadings powerful, look at them as secondary headlines, and write them as such. I personally don't, because it takes too much time. There are people who say I should, but I don't enjoy it, so I don't do it.

I like to keep my subheadings short, clear, and to the point. For example, if I'm writing a post for my tomato blog called "5 Mistakes That Will Ruin Your Tomato Plants," the subheadings could be:

1. Forgetting to Water
2. Not Using the Proper Water
3. Not Having Enough Light
4. Wrong Nutrition
5. Bugs, Bugs, Bugs

Nothing fancy. Just straightforward subheadings. I could probably keep some people reading for longer if I had more enticing subheadings, but I don't mind. The people who really need the information will keep reading.

3. Highlight Important Parts

Next, you can highlight sentences, words, or whole paragraphs. This is mainly done via **bolding** or *italicizing*.

I like to **bold important parts** of my blog posts. This **allows your readers to get the gist of your article** without having to go through the whole thing.

Sometimes people scan your article before they read it all the way through, so it's good to cater both to those who read every word and those who scan.

Be careful of highlighting too much. The more you highlight, the more power your highlighting loses. It's like the boy who cried wolf. If you do it too much, it loses its effect.

How sparingly? Once per each subheading/section is a good guideline, or once every 4-5 paragraphs.

4. Leverage Bullet Points

Bullet points allow your reader to:

- Take in information quicker
- See which parts of the post are relevant to them

- Take a breather between large blocks of text

See how effective bullet points are? Use them when and where it makes sense. If you have a list, use bullet points or a numbered list. If you give short tips, use bullet points.

How many bullet points should you use? There is no hard and fast rule. Put yourself in your ideal reader's shoes and ask what would make his or her life easiest.

I'm sure you're familiar with the list post format, which in essence is a big list of bullet points. An example from my blog is: "21 Things You Can Do to Change Your Life Forever" (http://www.wakeupcloud.com/change-your-life/).

5. Use Images (And Captions)

Images break up content, and they give you an opportunity to use captions (the text below an image). Captions are powerful, so use them to build up curiosity and to keep people reading.

The next time you read a newspaper or a blog that uses images with captions, note how your eye is drawn to the image, then to the caption below the image, and then to the rest of the page.

You don't have to restrict yourself to just using an image in the beginning of your post. You can use images for every sub-heading if you want to. The downside is that it takes time to find images, so you may want to restrain yourself.

If you want to find great, free images, check out Flickr.com or Unsplash.com. If you use Flickr, you can limit your search to Creative Commons-licensed images, which means you'll find images that you can use for free on your blog (if you link back to the original image). You can use as many images as you want as long as you include attribution.

I tend to use an image at the top of my posts. There are times when I'll use more than one image in a post, but usually I don't, because once again, it takes a lot of time for me to find good images, and I'd rather spend that time doing what I enjoy, which is writing more content.

Could you get by without images? Sure, but chances are it will lower the amount of interest you get on your posts. So I recommend you use one image at the beginning of your posts and go from there.

6. *Stay on Topic*

Staying on topic means that every paragraph you write should add value to your post. Each word should give Steve what you promised him in your headline.

This is not a life or death situation, so don't take this too seriously. You're allowed to go on a rant if you feel like it, but remember that the fewer words you can use to convey a message, the more likely that people will read it.

You don't have to share every single detail that seems related to your current topic. You just have to fulfill the promise you make in your headline.

With each sentence, ask yourself:

- Do people have to know this?
- Do I have to write this to fulfill the promise in my headline?
- If I remove this, will it matter?

If the answer is no, remove it.

For instance, if I'm writing an article called "5 Mistakes Beginning Bloggers Make," I only have to share five mistakes. This is where things get hazy, because I could just tell people the mistakes and leave it there, but that wouldn't be very valuable.

What I do is share the mistakes I've made and (briefly) what I learned from making that mistake and how I got out of it. The amount of detail I go into will depend on how long I want my post to be.

With each sentence I write, I try to ask myself, "Is this relevant? Does this help my reader?"

There is no formula I can give you for staying on topic, because there are times where you can help your reader further by going on a tangent, and there are times where you need to delete 50% of your post.

Knowing what to do will come from reading and writing a lot. It will come as you make mistakes and gain experience.

This is Obvious, Right?

You may think, "Henri, c'mon, this is so obvious a fourth grader could do it."

I agree, this is obvious, but most people don't write this way, because learning to write scannable posts takes work. It's much easier to dismiss this as obvious and then publish post after post that's not up to standard.

There's nothing revolutionary here, but are you breaking up your content? Do you make sure you stay on topic when you write? Do you use simple language? If not, then it's time you mastered the fundamentals.

Many bloggers want to skip right to the advanced stuff. They believe they'll succeed faster if they do, but it is only through putting in the work and learning the basics that you will succeed.

Action Step

Pick one tip from above to focus on when you write your next blog post. If you have trouble writing short paragraphs, make it your goal to experiment with it.

Once you're done, pick another tip, and move through the list. After a while, you will have gone through all six tips, and your readers will rejoice.

Plan Your Posts

What if I told you that you could double or triple your writing speed while improving the quality of your posts?

You don't have to believe me, because I recently coached someone on my podcast, and they were able to improve their writing speed by 300%. You can listen to the episode here: http://www.wakeupcloud.com/11/.

If you want to write faster, you have to plan better. You have to structure your posts before you start writing. That means you have to outline.

If you don't, you run the risk of rambling, going on tangents, and eventually throwing away the whole post, or worse yet, having to spend hours rewriting and editing.

Outlining is my secret weapon. It is what helped me write thousands of articles and millions of words in the time I've made a living online.

In this chapter you'll discover how I outline my blog posts, books, products, and courses. Let's dive right in, shall we?

The Power of Planning

Planning before you write will not only help you stay on track, but also write faster. When you plan, you will know what points you need to cover, and you will know when you're going off track.

This allows you to freewrite the first draft of your post. Freewriting simply means writing as fast as you can without trying to edit while writing. If you try to edit and write at the same time, you will fry your brain. The symptom of brain burnout is frustration, overwhelm, and despair. Sound familiar?

Outlining doesn't just help you write blog posts readers love, it can help you create any kind of content, such as podcasts, videos, courses, programs, or books.

1. Start With a Promise

I start with the headline. You've already learned how to craft a compelling headline in a previous chapter so I won't go into that here.

The headline gives me something I can look at and ask, "Is my outline in line with what the reader will expect?"

Your headline sets an expectation, and the job of your outline (and post) is to fulfill that expectation, and if possible, exceed it. Exceeding it is what will leave your reader delighted.

To keep this concrete, let's use an example throughout this chapter. Let's imagine I'm writing an post called "How to Start Growing Tomatoes Even If You've Never Touched a Plant."

2. Create Your Main Outline

After I've got my headline figured out, I figure out the subheadings, and I start with questions like:

- What?
- Why?
- When?
- How?
- What if? (objections)
- Mistakes?
- Examples?

This gives me an idea for how I want to write my post. In this particular case, the expectation I'm setting is that when you read my post, you'll learn how you can get started growing tomatoes. You have no previous knowledge, but you're willing to learn.

I have several ways I could write this post. I could make it comprehensive, or I could make it quick and easy. I'll go for the latter.

Next, I'll plan my subheadings, or my main outline, which might look something like this:

Introduction
Tomatoes are easy
3 steps to getting started
What to avoid
Conclusion

Once I've got my outline in place, I'll look at my headline and ask myself if this meets the expectations I've set with my headline. In this case, I only have to tell the reader how to get started, which I do with my 3 steps in the middle of the post. The rest is gravy.

3. Fill in the Details

Once I'm satisfied with my main outline, I'll outline each subheading. Imagine that each subheading is a mini blog post and it'll make more sense.

Here's what my final outline might look like:

Introduction
- Growing tomatoes can seem hard
- You can end up ruining everything if you don't get things right

- But getting things right isn't so hard
Tomatoes are easy
- I started off not knowing anything
- Eventually I figured things out
- You can do it, too
3 steps to getting started
- Pick the right seeds
- Get the right equipment
- Prepare the soil
What to avoid
- Low-quality seeds
- Low-quality soil
Conclusion
- This doesn't have to be hard
- Step-by-step does it
- Experiment

As you can see, I know nothing about growing tomatoes, but this will give you a sense of how I put an outline in place that keeps my post laser-focused.

This saves me time, because I don't have to rewrite my post over and over again for it to make sense. I can see if things go off track in the outline.

Now that I've got a detailed outline in place, I can start writing.

4. Freewrite

My definition of freewriting is writing without stopping. Sometimes I'll use a kitchen timer to challenge myself to write a first draft of a post in 20 minutes.

Once I have an outline in place, I know where my post is going, and I know the points I need to cover.

When I first began freewriting my posts, I worried about putting gibberish on the page, but what I realized is that I'm not going to publish the first version of my post. I'm going to come back and edit and rewrite a few times.

Freewriting simply allows me to dump everything I know into my document. It's much easier to rewrite once I have all my ideas down.

If you've never tried freewriting, you may resist it at first. But remember, writing isn't about producing the perfect blog post on the first try. It's about having a writing process that takes you from a blank document to a published post that readers love.

If You Get Stuck

If I ever find myself stuck, I imagine my ideal reader interviewing me. For my tomatoes post, the questions might look something like this:

- What shouldn't I do?
- Why should I grow tomatoes?
- How do I get started?
- What equipment do I need?
- Do I need a certain kind of soil?
- What kind of seeds should I buy?
- Should I read any books? If yes, where should I start?

And so on. I might also visit a few forums, blogs, or read a few articles on the topic and see what the most common problems are.

In other words, I do what I have to do to move the post forward.

Do Not Pass Go

When I help people write faster and better, the first thing I ask is, "Do you outline before you write?"

The usual answer is no.

People "just" write. They expect perfection to flow out of their fingertips, but it doesn't work that way.

You need structure, so remember to outline and plan your posts before you begin writing, and when you do begin writing, remember to freewrite your first draft.

Action Step

Create an outline for one of your future posts. You could even create a fake blog post to practice on. Pick a topic you know well, write a compelling headline, create a detailed outline, and freewrite.

You'll notice that when you get an outline in place, it almost pulls you in, making you want to start writing right away. Welcome to the world of outlining. You'll never look back.

Leverage Proven Templates

Humanity hasn't changed much in terms of how we're influenced or what we like. That means that templates work, and they work beautifully.

Templates make your life easier. You don't have to figure out everything from scratch, instead you can use the boundaries of a template to be free to experiment.

I've kept the amount of templates in this chapter to four to reduce overwhelm. You can go a long way with just these four templates.

I also have something in store for you at the end of this chapter that I think you'll like. Before we go there, let's look at the four templates.

1. The How-To Post

The how-to post is a classic. It's popular and attractive because it promises to teach you something valuable. The structure of a how-to post looks something like this:

Introduction
What (define the problem)
Why (benefits of learning this)
How
Mistakes (what not to do)
Examples
Summary

You can add or remove pieces as needed. For example, at times you may just want to write a short how-to post, in that case, all you'd need is the introduction and how-to part. It's up to you to decide what your readers need and what's appropriate.

To give you an example, let's return to our tomato blog. The article we're writing is "How to Stop Snails from Eating Your Tomato Plants." Now, I don't know if snails pose a threat to tomato plants, but let's pretend that they do.

Here's what an outline might look like:

Introduction - My Battle with Snails
What - The Problem with Snails

Why - Why Snails Like Tomato Plants
How - 3 Steps to Stopping Snails
Mistakes - 3 Mistakes You Should Avoid
Examples - A Story of How I Stopped Snails
Summary

As you can see, the how-to post is simple to write. It can also be modified in many ways. You'll see what I mean when we get to template #3: the comprehensive guide. The bottom line is that you can put in or take out any element as long as you fulfill the promise you make in your headline.

Always put yourself in your ideal reader's shoes and you'll do just fine.

Let's take another example, this time from writer and author Jeff Goins: "How to Overcome Writer's Block" (http://goinswriter.com/how-to-overcome-writers-block/). The post goes something like this:

Introduction (problem included)
Causes of writer's block
How to vanquish writer's block
Creative solutions

What I recommend you do is think about what questions your ideal reader wants answered, and answer them in your post.

A common pitfall is to start chasing the perfect formula, the perfect way to write a how to post. That formula doesn't exist. If you look for perfection, you forget about your ideal reader. You'll be unsure of if you're doing this right. Don't worry, worrying is normal. Just focus on your ideal reader and do your best.

2. The List Post

The list post is great for attracting traffic and social shares. List posts work well because they promise valuable information in bite-sized pieces.

A list post is the fast food of online content, but not as unhealthy. It's convenient and easy to consume, and unlike fast food, it nourishes you (when done right).

List posts are a fun and easy to write. The structure looks like this:

Introduction
Point 1
Point 2
Point 3
Conclusion

You can add more, but that's what a list post is when it's stripped down to its essentials. To give you an example, let's look at one of my more popular articles, "21 Things You Can Do to Change Your Life Forever"
(http://www.wakeupcloud.com/change-your-life/).

Here's the structure:

Introduction
Point 1
Point 2
And so on until point 21

That's it. I didn't even include a conclusion or summary, I simply wrapped up the post with the last point. Each point on the list was around 50-80 words. That post alone has gotten thousands of visitors and has been shared hundreds of times.

Each point should tie to your headline, so if I'm writing a post for my tomato blog called, "11 Mistakes You Have to Avoid When Growing Tomatoes," what I'd have to do is list 11 mistakes. That's all I have to do to fulfill the promise in the headline.

If I'm writing about mistakes, I like to include how the problem can be alleviated. It could be a sentence or two that hints at the solution. There is no real structure needed to each point. Sometimes I'll give straight up advice, and sometimes I'll tell a story. Whatever I do, I make sure to tell my reader about one mistake they have to avoid.

At times I'll go deeper into one point, but I try not to. If I want to go deeper, I write another article and link to that article from my list post. I try to keep my list points symmetrical, meaning that each point is roughly equal in words to every other point.

3. The Comprehensive Guide

When I want to target a keyword, attract links, and delight my readers, I write a comprehensive guide. For example, a guide I wrote is called "How to Start a Blog - The Ultimate Guide" (http://www.wakeupcloud.com/how-to-start-a-blog/).

In it I detail exactly what you need to do to get a self-hosted blog up and running. I recommend web hosts, themes, and other services that I personally use.

When I'm writing a guide like this, I like to look at what other bloggers have written about the topic. Then I write down what they're missing. I look at their comments and I jot down what questions are left unanswered. I'll try to figure out what's missing from the post and how I can make mine better.

So with my how to start a blog guide, here's the outline:

Introduction (and what you'll learn)
Why you should start blogging today
The most important factor for building a popular blog
How to get a domain name
How to come up with a great domain name (3 tips)
3 reasons you should start a self-hosted blog
3 reliable web hosts I recommend
How to choose your web host
How to get set-up (video)
The premium WordPress theme I use
5 mistakes you should avoid
Takeaway

While writing a comprehensive guide may seem overwhelming, I like to look at it as many smaller articles put together. You may have to work on it for a few days, but the effort will be worth it.

4. The Resources Post

A resource post is all about rounding up resources. It could be the 5 best podcasts in your niche, or the 7 best blog posts on getting started knitting.

You're linking out to people, which will not only provide value to your readers, but can also help you get noticed by the people you're linking out to.

The structure of a resource post is similar to a list post, but instead of having different points, you have different resources. What I like to do is briefly explain why I like each resource and how to use it, then I link to it.

An example of this is my article "5 Podcasts That Will Help You Build a Thriving Lifestyle Business" (http://www.wakeupcloud.com/5-internet-business-podcasts/).

The outline looks like this:

Introduction
Podcast 1
Podcast 2
... Podcast 5
A note on overwhelm
Over to you (ask if I've missed a podcast)

Are you starting to notice a common pattern in these templates? They are straightforward and simple. They are like Legos—you can add or remove parts to create what you need.

You might worry that you'll lose readers by sending people away to other sites, especially if someone is visiting your site for the first time. My answer to that is to focus on helping your reader.

Yes, sometimes you may send someone away, but it doesn't matter. You should always put your reader first, and that may at times mean sending them to someone else.

Even if people go to another blog and forget yours, they may bump into your blog again in the future, and they'll be more likely to stay because they remember that they've been to your blog before, and that you helped them.

A Small Surprise

I have a small surprise in store for you at the end of this book. I've compiled the templates in this chapter, and a few more, into a workbook that you can print out. The workbook will help you use these templates for your own blog.

For now, play with these, look at the examples, and make them your own. Don't worry about following the templates exactly. Use them as a springboard for your own posts.

If you fall into the trap of wanting to follow the templates exactly, just notice the tendency and stop. You won't write blog posts your readers love by becoming a robot. Your readers want you to help them, so focus on your ideal reader, and share relevant stories that will help, inspire, and educate.

Action Step

The action step I want you to take is not to write a whole blog post, unless you feel like it, but to pick one template, look at one example, and then create an outline for a future blog post.

Don't take it too seriously. Don't worry about following the templates exactly. Play with them and see what happens. The more you practice, the better you'll get. Forget about perfection, and focus on gradual improvement.

Have a Writing Process

Do you know the key to becoming a prolific writer? It's quite simple: Write like you're insane. Challenge yourself to write as quickly and as horribly as you can (after you've outlined your article).

Writing blog posts that your readers love is not just about writing and hitting publish sixty minutes later. If you want to write posts that get loved, shared, and commented on, you need a writing process.

My writing process has taken years to develop. I didn't always write as I do now, and mind you, I'm still improving each and every day.

Having a writing process means you have a ritual for how you write. It means you go through a step-by-step process for getting a blog post done.

Once it's ingrained, it becomes as easy as putting on your clothes in the morning and brushing your teeth.

Using Your Brain to Write Better

The fewer things your brain has to think about, the more energy you have left to produce great blog posts.

A writing process helps you save energy, because you know what you need to do next, how you need to do it, and when.

It minimizes overwhelm, because you don't have to get your blog post perfect on the first try. A house isn't built without a blueprint. You need a plan, and you need checklists. That's exactly what a writing process gives you.

Here's my writing process:

1. Outline

You already know how to get a headline and an outline done, so we won't go into that here. Almost every blog post, product, or course that I create begins with an outline.

The outline—headline included—is what keeps me on track. It ensures that I fulfill the promise I make in my headline.

An outline doesn't just have to be a list in a document. It could also be a mind map. There's no one way to outline, so feel free to find what works for you. What matters is that you flesh out the structure of your article before you begin writing.

Your outline is what will reveal—before you begin writing—what you need to cut out and what you need to add.

2. Write Horribly

After you've got an outline in place, your job is to fill that outline with horrible writing. Don't even try to write well. Dump your mind on paper. Forget about grammar, mistakes, flow, and anything else.

When you write horribly, you'll run into resistance. You'll grit your teeth. You'll want to go back and edit. Whatever you do, resist that urge.

Focus on getting your first draft done as quickly as possible.

The more you practice writing horribly, the more you realize that you can't produce perfection right off the bat. Creativity isn't linear, so you have to allow your brain to dump everything that is relevant into your post.

Later, you'll come back to rewrite and edit. That's when you can get picky and worry about grammar, but for your first draft, forget perfection and write like you're insane. Write like there are no rules.

When I'm not feeling up for writing horribly, what gets me unstuck is writing something, anything. I might write about how I hate writing. I'll explore my thoughts. I'll write "bla bla bla," and it'll loosen me up. The key is to simply write something. It'll trick your brain into writing mode.

To challenge myself, I'll use a kitchen timer set for 20-25 minutes, and I'll do nothing but write until the timer goes off. If you want more information on using time blocks like this, look up the Pomodoro Technique.

In the beginning, writing horribly may not make much sense, but trust the process, and do it anyway. It'll make your writing faster and better, and in time, you'll come to love it.

3. Drop It

Once I've got my horrible first draft in place, I take a break for around 24 hours. After I've had a good night's sleep, I return with a fresh pair of eyes (and fingers).

The more of these 24 hour breaks I take, the better my blog post becomes. But I avoid ending up in perfection-land. I'll often rewrite a post twice. Let me give you an example. A typical schedule might look like this:

Monday: Come up with a headline, outline and write a first draft
Tuesday: Rewrite so things make sense
Wednesday: Rewrite and put in final touches
Thursday: Final check and publish

Many bloggers rush to publish their work. If they would only be willing to let their posts mature, it would immediately increase the quality of their work.

When you take your 24 hour break, what do you do? You could outline other posts, focus on other tasks, or take a walk. It's up to you. What matters is that you let your post sit for at least 24 hours.

4. Rewrite

Once I've rested for at least one night, I come back and I rewrite my blog post. Sometimes this means rewriting the whole post, and sometimes it just means I do a few quick edits.

It really depends on how horrible my horrible first draft is. Rewriting my whole post isn't as hard as writing it from scratch, because I now have something to work with. I have the idea of the post, and I see where it's going, I just have to tidy it up.

When I rewrite, I start reading my post from top to bottom, and when I come across something that I feel could be improved, I stop and rewrite. If I need to rewrite a whole sentence, I'll start a new sentence above the old sentence, and when I'm done, I'll remove the old sentence completely, replacing it with the new one.

If I just need to change a few words here and there, I'll do it without writing a whole new sentence.

These are a few example of how I do things. As I said earlier, the more you do this, the more you'll find your own way of writing, rewriting, and editing, so what this comes down to is putting in the time and being okay with things not being perfect.

There is no perfect way to write. You'll find what works through writing oodles and oodles of blog posts.

Bye Bye Perfection

My writing process allows me to minimize perfectionism and fear. I know that my goal is to write a horrible first draft, not to get a perfect post done right away.

I also give myself time to write. I try to avoid having to write and publish a post on the same day, because it means I'll be more likely to miss obvious mistakes. I have to give my brain time to think about my article.

When you apply this process, you'll see the quality of your work go up dramatically. In time, you'll get more of those thank you emails from readers that you love. This is the extra step most bloggers are unwilling to take.

Action Step

Your action step is to test this process in your blogging. Create an outline, write a horrible first draft, and then sleep on it (not literally, of course).

Come back the next day, tidy things up, and see what happens. I think you'll be pleasantly surprised. This will also help you eliminate a lot of the stress of blogging. You will have to schedule your writing a bit better, but it's worth it.

Avoid Blogger's Block

At some point, you'll get stuck. You'll run into a wall made exclusively for bloggers and writers. For some people, this wall stops them from moving forward. For others, they realize that there's a weak spot in the wall and they punch their way through.

I've been writing consistently since early 2009. I write even when I don't feel like writing. I'm sure you've wondered how some bloggers keep producing post after post, while others fade into obscurity. That's exactly what we'll cover in this chapter.

You see, it's not about not having problems or not struggling. It's about how you face the challenges on your path. When you're determined enough to keep moving forward, you will. But if you're looking for signs to stop, you'll find them.

Here are my secret tricks for beating blogger's (or writer's) block:

1. Lower Your Standards

Often when I get stuck, I'm trying to do too much. I'm trying to write a post that covers everything and pleases everyone. I'm trying to produce perfection before I've even started.

The solution? I lower my standards. I allow myself to write that horrible first draft. I allow myself to play with my headline, outline, and the rest of my writing. I don't take things so seriously.

This is even harder when you're making a living through your writing. There's all sorts of pressures that crush you like a bug, if you let them. The key, at least for me, is to focus on having fun. I write because I enjoy it. I blog because I love it. I'm writing this book because I'm passionate about seeing you move forward.

When I forget this, I get stuck. When I lower my standards, I allow myself to play. So when you get stuck, which you will, look at what standards you've set up for yourself. What do you expect? Then lower those expectations and enjoy your blogging, because that's why you started in the first place, right?

2. The Magic of Questions

When you write your posts, it can be tough to get into writing mode if you just use statements. I mentioned this briefly in the chapter on outlining, but let's take another look at it from a different angle. For example, an outline with statements might look like this:

Introduction
Why you should eat apples
How to eat apples
What kind of apples to avoid

When you turn those statements into questions, writing becomes easier. It becomes a conversation, and your ideal reader jumps to life. Here's what the same outline might look with questions:

Introduction
Why are apples good for me?
Is there a best way to eat apples?

Are some apples more toxic than others when it comes to pesticides?
Any other tips I should know about?

Do you notice how much easier it becomes to write? If I'm extremely stuck, I'll ask myself sub-questions under each question. We've gone through this in the outlining chapter, so you know this already.

All I do is start asking myself questions while focusing on my ideal reader. Try it, you'll like it. Blogging doesn't have to be a mystery. You don't have to change your address to Writer's Block Land. You can keep writing.

3. Steal

If for some reason I'm still stuck, I'll dip into ideas and feedback I get from my readers. But let's assume you don't have readers (yet). When I was starting out, I stole ideas from other bloggers.

I wouldn't plagiarize or do anything naughty. I would simply go to a popular blog in my niche, look at some of their most popular posts (you can usually find them in the sidebar), and see if they couldn't inspire me to write something on a similar topic.

A fear I had in the beginning was that I didn't want to write about what others had already covered. I got over that quickly, because I realized that my readers wanted to hear my perspective. They wanted me to touch on topics that had already been covered a million times, because no one had written about those topics in the way I did.

If you need more ways to come up with ideas, go back to the chapter on coming up with ideas.

Remember, there are no rules. When you run into the blogging wall, everything is game. You don't have to give up. You can go get a truck and drive right through the wall.

4. Identify Your Monsters

Last but not least, look at what you're afraid of. If you're still stuck, it's because you're keeping yourself stuck.

Maybe you're afraid of what people will think, what might go wrong, or that no one will read what you write.

It's normal to have worries and fears. The biggest bloggers in the world have them, myself included. If they say they don't, they're lying. The trick is not to try and get rid of your fears, but to focus on the present moment.

You can't control the future. You can only do your best right now. Besides, if you dwell on your worries, you'll never get another blog post written. Do your best to focus on the here and now, and write.

If you're having a particularly bad day, you might just need a break. When I have one of those days where everything seems wrong with the world, I take a break. I don't stress about trying to solve the riddle that is my life. I simply enjoy life to the best of my ability. I spend time with my son. I might watch a movie, read a book, or do whatever I feel like doing at the time.

I have to constantly remind myself that life is way too serious to take seriously. When I focus on why I blog (because I love it), things shift almost immediately.

The Bottom Line

While blogger's block, or writer's block, is common, it doesn't have to kill your blog. There are ways to get unstuck.

Sure, there will be times where writing is harder than usual, but you can still write. You just have to find your way out of your rut and start typing away.

Even on bad days, you can still have a conversation, you can still talk. That means that you can still write.

The best advice I can give is to write. If you feel stuck, write about your stuckness. Write in a journal, diary, or just an empty document that you later throw in the trash. Write without expectations and you'll feel better afterward.

Action Step

If you're stuck right now, pick one of the four tips above and apply it.

If you're not stuck, use tip #1 on lowering your standards. Look at what your expectations are. If you haven't started your blog yet, why not? Are you procrastinating because you aren't ready yet? Start anyway. The sooner you start, the sooner you'll get going.

Forget about standards. Forget about expectations. Start writing, even if you think your writing is no good. And remember to enjoy the ride.

Stay Motivated

We've covered blogger's block, but what about when you run out of steam? What about when you don't seem to have any energy to write?

Those times are tough. I've had days where I've wanted to throw in the towel, even though I have thousands of subscribers, and even though I get thank-you emails every single week.

We're human beings, which means our emotions go up and down. Our motivation ebbs and flows. It's natural. The more you fight it, the more you'll perpetuate the cycle. Our culture today is all about doing, achieving, and becoming. No one tells you that you have to relax and recharge. No one—except me of course.

There will be days when the last thing on your mind will be to blog. You have to prepare for those days, and you have to make a few mental shifts to get through these periods.

If you don't, you may give up before you've even given your blog the chance to succeed. Many bloggers give up in the first 6-12 months, which means they give up right before they start gaining traction.

Let go of the instant gratification mentality, and focus on doing the work, because that is when you'll see the results you're after, and that is when you'll start enjoying what's actually here now.

Here are four ways in which I stay motivated to blog, even when all I want to do is crawl under my bed covers and eat chocolate ice cream:

1. Set Non-Results Based Goals

Non-results based goals means setting goals you have control over. "Make $1,000 per month from my blog within 6 months," may seem like a goal you have control over, but you don't.

A better way would be to break that goal into the milestones needed to get there, such as:

- Doing one task per day to bring visitors to your blog
- Writing an ebook
- Launching an ebook

In other words, non-results based goals are more like habits. They are things you do every day that then lead to the end result.

It's easy to get caught up in constantly belaboring the fact that you've not yet reached your goal. That's why it's much more productive to focus on what you can do. The rest will fall in place when the time is right.

To stay motivated, I've learned to enjoy the journey and the hard work that goes into reaching a goal, because I've noticed that striving for something only makes me miserable. Even if I reach my goals, I'll set new goals. Life is lived between goals. Remember that.

So focus on the actions you can take everyday and you'll eventually reach your goals.

2. Prepare for Slow Times

Your motivation will go up and down, like a roller coaster, and often it isn't under your control. That's why you have to prepare for the times you don't have any energy to blog.

So how do you prepare?

You batch.

Instead of writing your one mandatory blog post for the week, write two or three. Instead of outlining one post, outline five. Challenge yourself to do more. Batch similar tasks. It will make things easier on your brain, because you don't have to switch from one task to another.

It takes time for your brain to refocus if you switch between tasks. This is why multitasking is so ineffective.

So when you're writing a blog post, try to write more than one. Set aside an hour to outline three posts instead of one. In a few weeks time of doing this, you'll build up a library of posts you can publish when you run out of steam and need a break.

Now, have I done this myself? Not as well as I should. You see, you don't have to be perfect. I'm not always motivated. I don't always batch. But I still keep writing. I keep moving forward no matter what.

The key is to not fight the ebb and flow of your motivation, but to flow with it. Prepare posts ahead of time if you can, but more importantly, keep writing. The more experience you gain, the more you will figure out what works for you.

3. Write Every Day

Set aside time everyday to write. You don't have to publish everything you write. Your writing doesn't have to be good. You just have to write.

I have to admit that I have times where I don't write every day. I don't worry about it. I don't berate myself. I do what feels best for me at the time.

But I do notice that when I write everyday, I write faster and better posts. I get going faster, and writing is more fun. Writing is like a muscle. The more you exercise it, even if you produce "crap," the better you get.

To write everyday, decide:

- When you'll write
- Where you'll write
- How you'll write
- How much you'll write

I don't have a set schedule for writing, but if you're the kind of person who does well with schedules, or who has trouble sticking to writing otherwise, choose either a time of day you write or a set word count.

For example, you might say that you write between 6AM and 7AM. Whatever happens, that's when you sit down and write. If nothing comes, you'll still sit there, and write bla bla bla on the page.

If you like having a word count instead, you could write 1,000 words per day. In his book, *On Writing*, Stephen King recommends 2,000 words per day.

You don't have to produce Pulitzer Prize winning prose. It just has to be words on a page.

4. Keep Blogging Lighthearted

Your motivation will take a nosedive if you take blogging too seriously. If your goal is to build a popular blog, or even to make money with your blog, do your best, but don't take it too seriously. Don't try to force results. Focus on non-results based goals.

When you write, allow yourself to play with the craft. Be creative and come up with new ways to express yourself. Above all, let yourself write crappy first versions of posts.

When you make it easy to start writing, you'll write, and you'll write a lot. If you're weighed down by a heavy cloud of seriousness, see if you can challenge yourself to write one paragraph about whatever comes to mind.

Getting started has always been toughest for me. It's like jumping in the water when you know it's cold. You hesitate and hesitate, but when you do jump in and swim around a bit, the water gets warmer and you start enjoying yourself.

To get over the hump, I focus on the smallest next step, which is to get started. It might be to write one sentence, or one paragraph, or even one word. It might even be to lower my standards, as I mentioned in the last chapter.

Whatever it is, I find that once I get started, things get easier.
As for jumping in the water faster, I just jump before I have the time to think about it.

Don't Fight the Flow

The more you try to fight the ebb and flow of motivation, the more exhausted you will become.

Let it be. Prepare for it, and do your best. That's all you can do.

There's no rush to get anywhere. You're here to enjoy life, so enjoy it. Have fun with your blogging and writing. Don't take it too seriously.

Action Step

Pick one tip in this chapter and apply it. If you like the idea of writing everyday, set a daily time for when you'll write.

Determine for how long you'll write or how many words you'll put on the page before you can get up, and then stick to it no matter what.

To avoid putting this off, start small. If you want to write every day, start by writing for just 5 minutes.

A Note on Success

If you aren't determined to blog, you'll probably give up before your blog gains traction. There's nothing wrong with that. But if you want to build a successful blog, you have to realize that it takes time. It takes time to learn how to write blog posts readers love.

It's only through first discovering what works and then putting in the work that you will succeed. There will be challenges. You will want to quit. You will freak out. But you can still reach your goals.

The key is determination. You have to be willing to keep moving forward when the going gets tough. The challenges are what shape you as a blogger. They are what contribute to your success, so embrace them for the gifts that they are.

The mistakes you make, and the challenges you overcome, you can share with your audience. They make for great blog posts.

Keep moving forward and you'll do just fine.
Listen to your inspiration and enjoy the ride.

Summary

Before we wrap this book up, let's do a quick recap of what you've just learned. Reading this recap will help cement the information in your brain, and it will make it easier for you to apply what you've learned.

Here's a quick summary:

1. Uncover Your Blogging Style

Stop looking for your blogging voice and start writing. Your voice will evolve the more you write. In the beginning, you'll hesitate and worry, but that'll pass as you write more. If you didn't get it yet, the message is: Write more and worry less.

2. Find Your Ideal Reader

Stop trying to please everyone and find one reader to focus on. This reader can change from post to post, but the overall theme of your blog stays the same. If your blog is about tomatoes, write about tomatoes. If you can, write to a past version of you. It's an easy way to get started.

3. Tell Inspiring Stories

To tell inspiring stories, you have to allow people to connect to you. Find a problem your audience has and find a story where you had that problem and solved it. Do that and you'll inspire your readers.

4. Generate Unlimited Ideas

Look at blogs, Q&A sites, books, capture your inspiration, tap into your past, and use the drill down method. If you apply any of these, you'll come up with more ideas than you can write about.

5. Craft Compelling Headlines

The headline is what will help your readers decide whether to keep reading or not. Make sure your headlines command attention. Start your swipe file and practice, practice, practice.

6. Write Scannable Posts

Make your posts easy to read by writing short paragraphs, using subheadings, **highlighting important parts**, using bullet points, and staying on topic.

7. Plan Your Posts

Outline before you start writing. It'll help you write faster and better blog posts. Start with the headline and then outline. Above all, remember to freewrite.

8. Leverage Proven Templates

Use the templates to craft blog posts that get shared and commented on. The how-to and list post are my favorites. And don't forget to check out the bonus at the end of this book.

9. Have a Writing Process

Write like you're insane. Forget about getting your post perfect on the first go. Once you've outlined your blog post, write a horrible first draft. Challenge yourself to write as "crappy" as you can.

10. Avoid Blogger's Block

We all get stuck. Expect it. When it happens, lower your standards, use questions, steal content ideas and identify your fears.

11. Stay Motivated

Your motivation will ebb and flow. When you prepare for it, your blog won't die a silent death. Set non-results based goals, write every day, prepare for slow times, and have fun. You blog because you enjoy it, so enjoy it.

Conclusion

You've reached the end of this book. We've covered a lot of ground, and you may be feeling slightly overwhelmed. Don't worry, it's just a sign that you're learning.

Give yourself a break and return tomorrow with a fresh brain. Once you start applying the techniques and tips in this book, you'll discover what works for you, and what doesn't.

Remember, you're not supposed to copy me, but to make this information your own. Take this book for what it is: A compendium of examples. This is how I blog. This is how I've written thousands of articles and millions of words. This is the writing that has helped me build a blog with thousands of subscribers.

Take what resonates with you and discard the rest. If you only take one thing from this book and apply it, it will have been worth it.

Now take action!

Bonus

I promised you a bonus with blog post templates you could print out. You can grab them at the following URL:

https://wakeupcloud.com/goodies/BlogPostTemplates.pdf

You don't have to sign-up for anything. All you have to do is go to the address above and grab it. If you want to share it with your friends, feel free to do so.

If for some reason the link doesn't work, email me right away at henri@wakeupcloud.com.

I hope you enjoy it!

Thank You

Thank you for reading this book. I appreciate it. If you have any questions, or would like to share your progress, I'm always one email away at henri@wakeupcloud.com.

I see all emails and try to reply to them as soon as I can. If you don't hear from me within 72 hours, please email me again because chances are that your email got lost in cyberspace.

I'd also like to ask that if you liked this book, and got something out of it, that you leave a review on Amazon, because it'll help this message reach more people and help them share their voices with the world.

Thank you for being a superstar and following your inspiration.

Connect

If you'd like to learn more about me, head on over to my blog at http://www.wakeupcloud.com/ and specifically my about page at http://www.wakeupcloud.com/about/

I also have a free newsletter where you get a free report (+ audiobook) when you sign-up. You also get content on a weekly basis that helps you move forward with your blog and make a living online doing what you love.

The newsletter is here:
http://www.wakeupcloud.com/newsletter/

You can also find me on Twitter:
http://www.twitter.com/henrijunttila

Or on Facebook:
https://www.facebook.com/WakeUpCloud

And as I mentioned earlier, if you have any questions, comments, or just want to say hi, feel free to email me at henri@wakeupcloud.com.

Printed in Great Britain
by Amazon